The
Hythe & Sandgate
Branch Line & Tramway

Peter A. Harding

H class 0-4-4T No.31521 with the branch train at Hythe Station on August 25th 1951. R.C.Riley

Published by

Peter A. Harding
"Mossgiel", Bagshot Road, Knaphill,
Woking, Surrey GU21 2SG.
ISBN 978 1 5272 8683 2
© Peter A. Harding 2021.
*Printed by Binfield Print & Design Ltd.,
Binfield Road, Byfleet Village, Surrey KT14 7PN.*

Contents

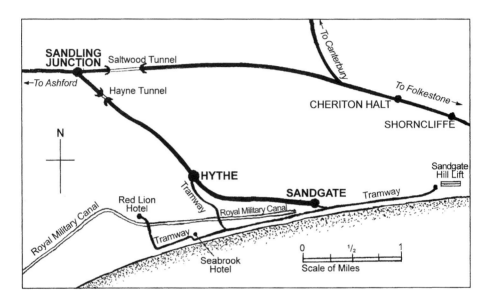

A wet day at Hythe as the branch pull-and-push train waits with D3 class 0-4-4T No.2365 at the station before returning to Sandling Junction in July 1938. R.F.Roberts

Introduction

People in the *Cinque Port town of Hythe in Kent and nearby Sandgate had hoped that when the railway reached their area they would soon be connected to the outside world and would become south coast holiday resorts to rival Eastbourne, Brighton and Bognor.

The coming of the railway would no doubt have been of great benefit to the development of both Hythe and Sandgate but, unfortunately they had to wait until 1874 before they got their wish after the line from Ashford to Folkestone had completely passed them by when opened in 1843.

The whole area around Hythe has certainly had an interesting history, in 1808 as part of a defence against a possible invasion from Napoleon and to protect the nearby low-laying stretch of the Romney Marsh, the Royal Military Canal was completed from Seabook (between Hythe and Sandgate) to the west of Rye towards Hastings in Sussex. Also, at about this time a series of defensive 'Martello' Towers were built from Folkestone to Seaford in Sussex.

Once the railway to Sandgate via Hythe was opened in 1874, there were great hopes of continuing the line to reach Folkestone Harbour from along the coast which would be a far easier route than the already existing steeply graded harbour branch. Unfortunately, through various reasons this never happened and after it was cut back from Sandgate in 1931 the line became just a sleepy single track branch line running between Sandling Junction and Hythe until it closed completely on December 3rd1951.

As a schoolboy at Ashford South School in the late 1950's the author was a member of the football and cricket teams who would sometimes travel from Ashford to play against Brockhill School at Saltwood, north of Hythe. On some occasions the team would travel by train from Ashford to Sandling Junction and then walk to Brockhill School which meant the odd glimpse of the trackbed and cuttings of the former branch line. These views would often get this Kentish schoolboy wondering what the line was really like.

*The Confederation of Cinque Ports is a historic series of coastal towns in Kent, Sussex and Essex. It was originally formed for military and trade purposes, but is now entirely ceremonial. The ports lie at the eastern end of the English Channel, where the crossing to the continent is narrowest.

A train waits at the remaining branch platform at Sandling Junction Station on August 25th 1951. At this time the double track branch line had been reduced to single track and cut back to Hythe only. R.C.Riley

3

History of the Line

While the South Eastern Railway (SER) were completing their new line from Redhill in Surrey to Ashford in Kent they were soon looking to continue towards the coast at Folkestone and Dover which were the nearest points to the continent. People in the coastal town of Hythe which at this time was considered a more prominent place than Folkestone must have thought there was a good chance that the new line would pass through or nearby and connect them with the ever growing railway network. Unfortunately this was not the case as on June 28th 1843 a temporary station was opened at Folkestone on the western side of Foord Valley bypassing Hythe and its neighbour Sandgate completely.

Both Hythe and Sandgate were at that time considered favourite places to visit and had high hopes of becoming the top health resorts on the south coast.

In a small way of compromise, a station was later opened between Ashford and Folkestone on February 7th 1844 and was called "Westenhanger and Hythe", but this small station was 3¹/₂ miles from Hythe and very much uphill.

As would be expected, the residents at both Hythe and Sandgate were not happy with this arrangement and soon complained to the SER who at that time seemed more involved with the construction work at Folkestone Harbour.

When the passenger service to the harbour was opened from Folkestone Junction on New Years Day 1849 the SER started to take more note of the complaints although nothing much happened. On April 1st 1852 Colonel Sandilands a local Hythe resident wrote to the SER asking them to seriously consider building a line to Hythe and Sandgate and, much to his surprise the SER answered by saying that they would ask their Chief Engineer Thomas Drane to survey for this new line.

After some months with very little happening, Mr.William Deeds (senior) the owner of Sandling Park Estate, with the backing of Colonel Sandilands, contacted the SER and suggested that the Westenhanger Station was moved to a more convenient site just north of Hythe, east of the Saltwood tunnel. This request was met with a similar response to the request for a branch line from the SER who announced that nothing could be done until a new road north from Hythe was completed, replacing a muddy lane.

Some three years later the hope for a branch line to Hythe and Sandgate still lingered on and the Mayor of Hythe, Thomas Deane called a public meeting at the Town Hall to drum up support for better railway communications. One person who quickly gave his view at the meeting was Mr.Raikes Currie, MP for Northampton and also a magistrate for Middlesex, Buckinghamshire, Essex, Hampshire and Kent who was living at the time in a rented house at Sandling Park. Mr.Currie mentioned that in his view nothing less than a branch line would be adequate. One suggestion which came from Mr.Henry Mackeson of the local brewery family was that in view of the recently opened Shorncliffe Military Camp near Sandgate, a new line could come in not from the Sandling Park direction but from the Folkestone direction and then extend to Hythe.

Even after all these requests still nothing happened until October 28th 1858 when Cornelius Eborall the SER General Manager passed a report to the board from a Mr. Knight suggesting the advantages of building a line from Westenhanger to Folkestone via Hythe and Sandgate to approach Folkestone Harbour from along the coast. This idea appealed to the SER as it would be a far easier route than the already existing steeply graded harbour branch.

4

The suggestion of this new route to Folkestone Harbour brought other similar ideas and one of these was a line from Cheriton running parallel to the main line and then down into the Foord Valley. The cost of this scheme proved too much and the idea was soon dropped although another scheme from Cheriton via the eastern part of Sandgate at Sandgate Hill and then along the Leas undercliff to the harbour did go before Parliament but received too many objections of which the most prominent one came from Lord Radnor who owned a large part of Folkestone.

Lord Radnor at that time was William Pleydell-Bouverie who was Viscount Folkestone until he became the 3rd Earl of Radnor on January 27th 1828 after the death of his father Jacob Pleydell-Bouverie. Despite their strong association with Folkestone, the Pleydell-Bouverie family seat was Longford Castle on the banks of the River Avon near Salisbury in Wiltshire although the 3rd Earl mainly lived at Coleshill House near Highworth in Berkshire where he had previously been MP for Downton from 1801 to 1802 before switching to Salisbury from 1802 to 1828.

Mr. Richard Hart, a local solicitor came up with a plan to build some of the line in a tunnel so that it did not interfere with Lord Radnor's land but after some consideration it was felt that this idea would prove too costly.

Another scheme for a line to include Hythe was put forward in August 1862 by some local landowners who planned to build a line through the Elham Valley from the London Chatham & Dover Railway (LCDR) at Canterbury to Hythe and would no doubt have the backing of the LCDR. But, even the thought of competition from their deadly rival company the LCDR failed to make much impression on the SER although as some form of compensation they did open a rather basic new station on the main line just west of Folkestone and gave it the title Shorncliffe & Sandgate even though it was about a mile from both places.

By February 1864 the SER were starting to think that at last they really should be building the line through Hythe to Sandgate (and no doubt hope that they could continue to Folkestone Harbour at a later stage) and their newly appointed chief engineer Francis Brady was sent to Sandgate to outline their plans. The route that the SER suggested was for the new line to leave the main line east of Saltwood Tunnel (although they later decided to leave to the west of the tunnel) and after passing Saltwood Castle, run along the back of Hythe where there would be a station then on to Sandgate where the station would be situated just below Shorncliffe Camp. This plan seemed to avoided most of the previous opposition and was authorised on June 23rd 1864.

By October 1866 the Hythe section of the Elham Valley scheme from Canterbury had been abandon and a few months later the whole Elham Valley scheme was dropped owing to financial difficulties.

The Elham Valley scheme was later revived by the SER in 1879 to connect Canterbury and Folkestone. It opened between 1887 and 1889 and closed in 1947.

With the original Elham Valley scheme dropped in 1866 the SER seemed to sink back into their rather relaxed attitude about Hythe and Sandgate where the local people must have given up hope of ever getting their railway.

A glimmer of hope came later in 1866 when the SER appointed Edward Watkin as their new chairman succeeding the Hon.James Byng. Watkin was a man of action who was involved with many railway companies both home and abroad and it came as no surprise when he was knighted in 1868 and was later made a baronet in 1880. He was also Chairman of both the Metropolitan Railway in the London area and the Manchester, Sheffield and Lincolnshire Railway and had for some time been involved in many ways of trying to work out a rail link from Liverpool and Manchester in the north of England via London and the south east to the Continent. Over the years Watkin looked at the possibilities of building a port at Dungeness so that a new cross channel steamer service between Dungeness and the French fishing port of Le Treport would then be shorter than any other route available. Also at a later date Watkin was very much involved with the Channel Tunnel Railway scheme which would certainly have given him his wish of a through connection to France.

During the early part of 1868 the SER even considered dropping the whole idea of the Sandgate line until they found out in August 1868 that there were two separate local schemes being put forward. Having listened to both schemes, the SER decided to back the one put forward by George Wilks, the Hythe Town Clerk who informed them that a gentleman called George Smith had organised a local group of people who were interested in forming a company to take over the SER's own powers of June 23rd 1864.

The name chosen for the new company was the "Hythe & Sandgate Railway Company Limited" (H&SR) and an arrangement between the SER and the H&SR was entered into in which the SER would lease and work the branch paying the H&SR a sum equal to $4\frac{1}{2}\%$ of the cost of the line and not exceeding £65,000.

On January 25th 1870 the H&SR were registered and comprised of seven directors: The Hon. James Bying, James Whitman (M.P. for Maidstone), Alexander Beattie, Henry Bean Mackeson, Gibson Hornan, Edward Leigh-Pemberton (M.P. for East Kent) and George Smith. The first meeting was held at the SER Headquarters at Tooley Street, South East London on March 3rd 1870 where it was decided that the H&SR would own the land of the new line with the SER providing the finance.

The last mile of the route to Sandgate would take up an elevated view of the English Channel which would soon attract seaside development. With this in mind the Seabrook Estate Company was formed with several directors of the H&SR also becoming directors of the new company.

At this stage the SER had high hopes that extending the line from Sandgate to Folkestone Harbour would still happen although at a SER board meeting in July 1871 Sir Edward Watkin reported that progress on the branch to Sandgate was still unsettled with one or two negotiation problems with the War Office over land at Seabrook still to be sorted out.

He also mentioned a scheme that had been put forward for a railway to run from Hythe to Ham Street on the northern side of the Royal Military Canal claiming that troops and stores from Hythe and Shorncliffe could be transported continuously to all parts of England, Scotland and Wales. The land along the side of the canal was owned by the War Office and the SER offered £40 per acre. This offer was refused by the War Office who said that they wanted at least £160 per acre. This news annoyed the rather quick tempered Watkin who was not happy dealing with the War Office and although discussions dragged on through the rest of 1871 the War Office were not prepared to drop their price and the whole scheme collapsed.

Powers to construct a 3 miles double track line from the main Ashford to Folkestone line at a point by the Sandling Estate to Sandgate via Hythe was included in a South Eastern Railway Act of 1872 and the person who was asked to cut the first sod of earth for the new line was none other than Prince Arthur, a grandson of Queen Victoria, who graciously consented to perform the ceremony.

The contract to build the line was awarded to Philip Stiff a Dover contractor at a price of £43,769.

The day for cutting the first sod of earth was set for Thursday April 11th 1872 and a special train left Charing Cross Station with Sir Edward and Lady Watkin, the Lord Mayor of London, the Sheriff of London plus directors and

Sir Edward Watkin
(1819 - 1901)
Author's Collection

6

officials of both the H&SR and the SER. The *London Daily News* mentioned in their Friday April 12th 1872 edition that the special train was driven in honour of the occasion by Alfred Mellor Watkin who later became the SER Locomotive Superintendent and just happened to be the son of Sir Edward Watkin. The train arrived at Shorncliffe Station not long before the Royal Train arrived from the other direction carrying HRH Prince Arthur and his entourage, Mr.C.W.Eborall the SER General Manager and many military officals from Dover.

The entire party then proceeded in a procession of horse drawn carriages through the streets of Sandgate to Hythe cheered all the way by what looked like the whole population plus many others from outside the area who decided to make a gala day with bunting and flags of all shapes and sizes along the whole route.

The ceremony of cutting the first sod of earth took place in a valley about half a mile outside of Hythe where it is believed that several thousand spectators had collected to watch this special event. The *Folkestone Express, Sandgate, Shorncliffe & Hythe Advertiser* reported in their Saturday April 13th 1872 edition as follows:-

The spectators cheered loudly as the Prince took the spade and made the first incision in the turf; but alas! and alack! so much was the strength of the handle of the spade reduced by the process of ornamentation, that it snapped in two under the pressure which His Royal Highness put upon it; renewed cheers, however, soon re-assured the Prince, and seizing the stump of the handle His Royal Highness speedily succeeded in raising the first sod and placing it in the barrow, which he wheeled a few yards along a plank and then overturned the sod, amidst tremendous cheering on all sides. Presentation implements may be very nice as souvenirs, but handsome as the spade was, it was evident that it was never intended for sheer hard work. Of course if there had been any one present opposed to the new line, this little contretemps of the breaking of the handle of the spade might have been twisted into an ill omen for the success of the undertaking; but the enthusiasm everywhere manifest forbade such a thought.

This illustration by the Victorian artist Edward Frederick Brewtnall (who at the time was working for *The Graphic* newspaper) clearly shows part of the broken handle laying on the ground while Prince Arthur carries on with the other part of the handle and silver spade. The Graphic

7

As soon as the formal turning of the first sod of earth was completed the contractor Philip Stiff lost no time in getting things moving and a body of men were soon at work at a cutting in a field close to Saltwood Castle.

Unfortunately, with the very nature of railway construction accidents happen and the following sad article appeared in the *Whitstable Times & Herne Bay Herald* Saturday April 19th 1873 edition as follows:-

HYTHE

The Accident on the New Railway Works - Fatal Result.

The unfortunate man William Griffey, who was severely hurt at the Saltwood cutting of the Hythe and Sandgate Railway on the 1st inst, succumbed to his injuries on Tuesday morning. He leaves a widow and six young children, including an infant born two days previous to the accident. An inquest on the body was held on Wednesday evening, in the Town Hall, before W.S.Smith, Esq., when the jury returned a verdict of "Accidental death".

With work on the construction getting under way, to speed things up, the gang of men employed to build the line were working night and day. Surprisingly the contract between Philip Stiff and the SER was not actually executed until July 31st 1873 and even then some of the land in the Seabrook area had still not been purchased from the War Office who wanted £350 per acre. Enventualy the some what reluctant Watkin agree to pay the sum of £1,981 17s 6d.

In January 1874 Francis Brady the engineer was asked when the line would be ready to be opened, to which he confidently gave an answer of May Day. Unfortunately with a land slip near where Hayne tunnel had been constructed, the work seemed to delay things to which Brady had to give a revised completion date of late June. As with many things involved with railway construction even this date was passed much to the annoyance of the impatient Watkin who had become MP for Hythe in February 1874 and wanted to open the line in the summer to attract high season visitors to the south coast. After Watkin had consulted with the directors of the H&SR concerning the contractor Philip Stiff, it was decided to get the SER workmen to finish the job. An agreement to release Philip Stiff from his original contract was reached whereby he accepted £6,500 and agreed to hand over all the equipment they were using to the SER to finish the work. When the work was finish the SER would then return everything to Philip Staff.

Once the SER navvies started working on the line, things soon got moving and the whole line was completed and ready for inspection towards the end of August. Colonel C.S.Hutchinson, the Board of Trade's Inspector of Railway's visited the line on August 29th but refused to sanction the opening to the public until a few details had been rectified which were mainly signalling at the junction and at Hythe and Sandgate stations. On September 24th the SER Secretary John Shaw informed his colleagues that he proposed that the formal opening would be on Friday October 9th and that he had mentioned this date to the Mayor of Hythe and that His Royal Highness the Duke of Teck would officiate at the ceremony. Fortunately on September 26th Colonel Hutchinson wrote that he had inspected the line once more and although there were still one or two things which needed attention, he was happy that the line could open on Friday October 9th 1874.

Having now got a date for the opening, the SER looked at the hope of extending to Folkestone Harbour and with this in mind sounded out Folkestone Corporation as to if they were willing to contribute but, this request was unsuccessful. They then approached Lord Radnor and no doubt with tongue in cheek asked him if he was prepared to let them have the land free of charge. As expected Lord Radnor rejected this request but did say somewhat surprisingly that he was not opposed to the railway but wanted to have the full price of the land. Once Watkin heard this news he recommended that this was not the right time to buy. On reflection this was probably one of the biggest mistakes that the forward looking Watkin made.

At this time Lord Radnor was Jacob Pleydell-Bouverie, 4th Earl of Radnor who had inherited the title after his father William Pleydell-Bouverie the 3rd Earl had died in 1869.

The big day for opening the railway to Sandgate had finally arrived and on Friday October 9th 1874 the people of Hythe and Sandgate must have thought that over the years this occasion would never happen. The day started overcast but the clouds soon moved away and the sun came out to shine on this great day. The *Dover Express* reported the opening of the new line in their Friday Octoner 15th edition as follows:-

OPENING OF THE HYTHE AND SANDGATE RAILWAY

The ceremony of opening the above railway, the first sod of which was turned in April 1872, by his Royal Highness Prince Arthur, was performed on Friday, by his Serene Highness the Duke of Teck. The arrangements of the day were entrusted to a Committee, consisting of the Mayor of Hythe (H.B.Mackeson,Esq.), George Wilks, Esq. (to whose exertions the formation of the branch-line is mainly due), J.Taylor,Esq., Messrs. J.V.Cobb, J.V.Bean, G.L.Grant, L.A.Loren, H.Scott, and J.Nelson, Mr. R.J.Sidle, to whose indefatigable energy and courtesy much of the success of the day were attributed, officiating as Hon. Sec. By the labours of this Committee a fund had been formed, by means of which the town was decorated in a manner which called forth the encomiums of all spectators. From the station to the Mayor's house, the road was fringed with masts bearing flags of every nation, and many which belonged to no ascertainable nation whatever. The house of the Mayor was most handsomely decorated with a profusion of fine cloth in black and red (the colours of the Duke of Teck), and many other houses in the town displayed great taste in their decorations. Numerous triumphal arches, festoons and strings of banners crossed the way, bearing such mottoes as "Welcome to Hythe", "Onward South Eastern Railway", "What a Day for Hythe", &c. The special train from Charing Cross, bearing his Serene Highness the Duke of Teck, the Right Hon.E.H.K.Hugessen, M.P.., Sir E.Watkin, M.P.., and Lady Watkin, the Hon.J.Byng, Mr.Shaw, Mr.Brady, and other officials of the South Eastern Railway, together with the principal guests invited, left Charing Cross at eleven a.m., arriving at Hythe shortly before one o'clock. After waiting a short time to take up passengers, it proceeded over the new branch to Sandgate, where after a short stay, during which the engine changed ends, it proceeded back to Hythe. The new station at Hythe was tastefully decorated with evergreens and flags, and on the down platform places were provided for the children of the National Schools, who, with banners and flags in their hands, awaited the arrival of a Serene Highness with a keenness of expectations most entertaining to the older spectators, to whom Royalty had lost somewhat of its pristine novelty. As the train entered the station the children and spectators generally set up a hearty cheer, and the band of the 82nd Regiment, which was present from Shorncliffe, played "Haydn's Hymn", the National Anthem of the Austrian Empire, of which Prince Teck is a born subject. As the Duke stepped on the platform, he was received by the Mayor and Corporation of Hythe, and Mr.R.J.Biron, the Recorder, read

Continued over page

The special train from London at Hythe on the opening day October 9th 1874. Illustrated London News

9

a loyal address, beautifully engrossed on vellum, and mounted in a red morocco case. His Serene Highness read a reply, in which he expressed his pleasure at being present on such an occasion, and the regret of his wife, the Princess Mary of Cambridge, that she was unable, owing to family reasons, to be there with him. He then declared the line to be open, upon which the company immediately left the station, and, entering carriages provided by the Corporation, proceeded in procession round the town, the route decorated as we have described, to a large marquee set up in the Corporation grounds, where a most elegant *dejenner* was served by Mr. Spencer, of the City Terminus Hotel, London, to which due attention was paid by a large and fashionable company, including, besides His Serene Highness the Duke of Teck, the Mayors of

Hythe, Dover, Folkestone and New Romney, the Right Hon. E. H. Knatchball Hugeseen, M.P., Sir Edward Watkin, M.P., Hon.J.Byng, Colonal the Hon. F.A.Thesiger, (commanding at Shorncllliffe). General Hankey, Revs.T.G.Hall, W.F.E.Knollys, Canon Puckle, &c., Lieutenant-Colonel Knocker,C.P.R.V., Capt.Sergeant, R.N., Alderman and Sheriff Ellis, the Under Sheriffs of London and Middlesex, and a brilliant assembly of ladies and gentleman, to whom the munificent hospitality of the Mayor and Corporation was extended.

The address being read to the Duke of Teck. The Graphic

The Friday October 9th 1874 edition of *The Globe* newspaper mentioned the following:-

The special train left Charing Cross Station at two minutes past eleven, in charge of Mr.Shaw (the general manager), the engine was driven by Mr. Alfred Watkin, son of the chairman. The train was fitted with continuous brakes. Travelling via Chislehurst, Tonbridge was reached at 11.45, Ashford at 12.30.

The junction of the new line with the old is near Sandling Park and about a mile past Westenhanger Station. The special train reached the junction at 12.50, and at once passed on to the new line under a row of flags which were suspended across it. Passing Saltwood Castle and crossing the fine valley beneath it, the train drew up at the new Hythe Station for a moment, and then went on over the remainder of the line to Sandgate Station, which forms the terminus of the line. The view from the embankment at this point is exceedingly pretty, reaching across Dungeness Bay, with Hythe church and town in the intermediate distances.

After a few minutes stay at Sandgate Station the train returned to Hythe, where upon alighting, the Duke of Teck and the visitors were received with loud cheering.

Sandgate Station in 1891, the original terminus of the new railway. Lens of Sutton

10

After the euphoria of the line opening, everything appears to have settled down well and with all trains starting from Westenhanger on the main line, the people of Hythe and Sandgate were happy to have their railway up and running after all the years of waiting.

The main thing on the minds of the SER was to reach Folkestone Harbour and they soon introduced a parliamentary bill for the 1876 session. The *London Gazette* of November 30th 1875 mentioned the following:-

In Parliament -Session 1876

South Eastern Railway Company

Extension of the Hythe and Sandgate Railway to Folkestone

NOTICE is herby given that the South Eastern Railway Company (hereinafter called "the Company") intend to apply to Parliament in the ensuing session for leave to bring in a Bill for this purposes or some of the purposes following (that is to say) -

To authorise the Company to make and maintain a railway, or some part or parts thereof, with all proper stations, approaches and works, commencing in the parish of Cheriton, in the county of Kent, by a junction with this Company's Hythe and Sandgate Branch Railway at the present termination thereof, and passing through and from this said parish into and through the parish and township of Folkestone, in the said county of Kent, and terminating in the said parish and township of Folkestone by a junction with the Company's railway in the Folkestone Harbour Station, at or near the south-eastern end of the new up passenger platform.

The aim was to continue as a double track railway from Sandgate Station (which was really at Seabrook and aimed at the future housing development) and move the station to a more central position in Sandgate. After 138 yards from the existing station, the line would enter a 310 yard tunnel which would curve slightly inland and have a 55ft retaining wall on the southern side. From the tunnel the line would continue through a deep cutting for 210 yards before entering another tunnel which would be 961 yards long. On leaving the tunnel the line would reach the centre of Sandgate before crossing over a massive 396 yard viaduct containing 36 arches. To build the viaduct would mean the demolition of Sandgate Castle and many properties. From here the line would then follow the coastline running alongside the Lower Sandgate Road for just over a mile before turning slightly inland and entering yet another tunnel, this one would be 608 yards long and would run underneath "The Leas" a unique clifftop promenade at Folkestone. After leaving the tunnel the line would then sweep round to the right and run into the harbour station.

The station staff on the 'up' platform at Hythe awaiting a train from Sandgate in 1904. Lens of Sutton

There was as much opposition in the Folkestone area (mainly led by Lord Radnor) to the extension as there was enthusiasm for it from the SER. A special public meeting was called by John Sherwood the Mayor of Folkestone on February 2nd 1879 where the views from both sides were heard although the opposition mainly boycotted the event, but made sure that enough posters were pasted up all around the town saying that the extension would spoil Folkestone and the railway would cut the town off from the beach.

While the debate over the extension to Folkestone went on for some time, the branch line to Sandgate carried on in its normal way and, although both stations were not really sited that well, the early days seemed quite successful. Hythe in particular was doing well where the new Seabrook Hotel which was owned and managed by the SER was opened on July 21st 1880, while troops from Shorncliffe Camp were now using Sandgate Station.

In the Saturday March 19th 1881 edition of the *Folkestone Express, Sandgate, Shorncliffe & Hythe Advertiser* the following interesting article appeared:-

THE HYTHE AND SANDGATE RAILWAY

It is reported that negotiations are on foot for purchase of the land requisite for the making of a line from Lydd and New Romney to Hythe, Sandgate and Folkestone. An engineer employed by the South Eastern Railway has been recently engaged in stumping out the land for the extension of the Hythe and Sandgate Railway to Folkestone Harbour. Tenders for contracts will shortly be issued, and the work commenced at once. We understand that the difficulty with regard to Sandgate Castle has been overcome.

Where this article mentions that 'the difficulty of Sandgate Castle has been overcome' it refers to the fact that the SER had actually bought the castle from the War Office for £20,000.

After the sea wall and Hythe Marine Parade had been completed in 1881, HRH the Prince of Wales was invited to perform the opening ceremony as well as laying the foundation stone for the extension of the new pier at Folkestone Harbour.

On Wednesday October 12th 1881 HRH the Prince of Wales arrived on a special royal train at Hythe Station accompanied by Sir Edward Watkin and other senior SER officials. In a similar way to the time when Prince Arthur turned the first sod of earth for the new railway in 1872 and the Duke of Teck performed the opening ceremony in 1874, the people of Hythe once again brought out the flags and bunting to make this yet another royal occasion to remember.

Having arrived at the station to much cheering, the Prince then made his way to a waiting open top carriage accompanied by Sir Edward Watkin, which was pulled by four fine horses and, followed by many other carriages of special guests travelled down Station Road with crowds of cheering people lining the streets. After passing along the Marine Parade which was then renamed 'Princes Parade' the entourage reached Sandgate and then on to Folkestone Harbour where the SER Chief Engineer Francis Brady presented the Prince with an ivory mallet to knock in the ceremonial stone.

Dignitaries and staff on the 'down' platform at Hythe, believed to be awaiting the arrival of the Prince of Wales on October 12th 1881. Miss Eva Fright Collection

12

The *Folkestone Express, Sandgate, Shorncliffe & Hythe Advertiser* of Saturday October 15th 1881 reported the special day and mentioned the following optimistic view:-

On one banner as it fluttered we caught the words "Success to the Hythe and Sandgate Railway. We are looking forward to the Sandgate and Folkestone Extension now, and closer union of the three towns".

With still nothing actually happening on the extension from Sandgate to Folkestone Harbour (even though an application in 1879 had been received to extend the time to the South Eastern Railway Act of 1876), the SER were somewhat concerned when they heard that the LCDR who were building their Maidstone to Ashford railway were surveying in the Ruckinge area (just south of Ashford) with a view to extending their line on to the Romney Marsh and possibly to Hythe. Sir Edward Watkin and James Staats Forbes the LCDR chairman were bitter rivals and the SER and the LCDR had often built lines purely as a defensive measure to stop entry into each others territory.

The *Folkestone Express, Sandgate, Shorncliffe & Hythe Advertiser* of Saturday April 14th 1883 reported the some what disheartening news as following:-

THE HYTHE AND SANDGATE RAILWAY EXTENSION OF TIME REFUSED

The Committee of the House of Commons, presided over by Mr.Hardcastle, resumed last Thursday the consideration of the South Eastern Railway Company Bill for the revival of powers as to the purchase of land for the extension of the Hythe and Sandgate Branch Railway to Folkestone. The clause for the revival of the powers as to the Hythe and Sandgate Branch Railway was opposed by Lord Radnor, and was eventually struck out of the Bill.

With rumours going around about the LCDR pushing not only towards Hythe (from the Ashford area) but also Folkestone from the Alkham Valley line promoted to run from Kearsney on the main LCDR Victoria to Dover line, Sir Edward Watkin felt that he should set out in 1884 other SER possibilities which included the latest position of the shafts for a Channel tunnel which had started in 1880-81 at first Abbot's Cliff and then Shakespeare Cliff both between Folkestone and Dover. Other possible new lines included again looking at a line linking New Romney and Sandgate and also a line extending north from the station at Sandgate via Shorncliffe Military Camp to join up with the main Ashford to Folkestone line at Shorncliffe Station.

Still hoping that the extension to Folkestone Harbour would one day happen, the SER in 1886 began planning a new station at the junction where the branch left the main line at the Sandling Estate. Local trains for Hythe and Sandgate had all started at Westenhanger the first stop from the junction on the main line towards Ashford

An early view of the 'up' platform at Sandgate.   Author's Collection

so it was felt that a station at the junction would be of great benefit. Although the area where the new junction station was to be built was sparsely populated, it was to have interchange facilities and all the branch services would start from the new junction instead of Westenhager. The new station was appropriately named Sandling Junction and was opened to the public on January 1st 1888.

Hythe Town Council were really pleased with the new station at Sandling Junction and wrote to the SER board and thanked them and mentioned that the general opinion was that Hythe could look forward to a brighter future and even had plans for a pier to be built from the Princes Parade.

The winter of 1891 produced one of the worst for many years and even included on March 10th the last train from Charing Cross to Sandgate getting stuck in a snowdrift near Saltwood Castle and the passengers stranded in the train all night until they were rescued the following morning by a local farmer.

In the same year on May 18th the first part of the new Hythe & Sandgate Tramway opened between the Seabrook Hotel and the east side of Sandgate. (*see pages 27 to 31 for details covering the tramway*).

During the latter part of 1898 the SER ended their rivalry with the LCDR (after Sir Edward Watkin had retired in 1894) by negotiating an arrangement whereby both companies remained separate but would work together from January 1st 1899 under the heading of the South Eastern & Chatham Management Commities (SE&CR).

Sandling Junction with a main 'up' train on the left and the branch train on the right. Author's Collection

Under the SE&CR the branch continued as before and some of the improvements which the SER had planned were soon carried out by the SE&CR.

A tragedy took place on Midsummer's Day 1899 at Sandling Junction when a traction engine crashed over the parapet of the road bridge over the main line on the approach to Sandling Junction from Westenhanger. The traction engine which belonged to a Mr.Padgham of Kingsnorth near Ashford was being driven by Henry Abbott and his steersman George Bingham. Although George Abbott was able to jump clear, the unfortunate George Bingham was not so lucky and went over the parapet where he lost his life after he was crushed under the wheels of the engine.

Another unfortunate event happened at Sandling Junction on April 2nd 1900 when the stationmaster Mr.Edward Hilder was run down by an 'up' express just a few yards from his house.

On April 23rd 1900 a troop ship returned to the docks at Southampton from the Boar War in South Africa, carrying many wounded soldiers who boarded a train bound for the station at Sandgate, which was the nearest point to Shorncliffe Camp. As word got around, many local people joined Civic and Military officials to greet the returning soldiers at the station giving them a heroes welcome and were joined by 80 stretcher bearers from Shorncliffe Camp. 115 wounded men were transferred from the station by horse buses to Beach Rocks Convalescent Home in Sandgate.

After the retirement of stationmaster George Wood in 1921, Sandgate Station came under the jurisdiction of Hythe and this was probably the first sign that the SE&CR were beginning to feel that without any extension to Folkestone Harbour, the station at Sandgate had served its purpose and even more so when the engine shed closed on December 31st 1921.

At the time of the railway grouping in 1923, the newly formed Southern Railway inherited all the SE&CR lines and the future of the Hythe & Sandgate branch seemed to be one branch which they quickly looked at.

Hythe Station looking north towards Sandling Junction.   John Alsop Collection

A fine view of Sandgate Station (which was really at Seaview) with the eastern end of the Royal Military Canal just behind the station.   Author's Collection

15

The past hopes of Sir Edward Watkin of a railway or tramway between New Romney and Hythe were of course never to materialise although, in 1927 the two places were connected when the Romney, Hythe & Dymchurch Light Railway built their 15 in gauge line under the Light Railway Act and then extended it along the coast to Dungeness two years later.

With the competition of road transport In 1930 the Southern Railway gave notice of their intension of closing Sandgate Station and the Friday November 7th edition of the *Dover Express* mentioned the following:-

SANDGATE STATION TO CLOSE

The Southern Railway Company has intimated to the Sandgate (Kent) Council that, as a result of serious loss from road transport competition, Sandgate Station is to be closed from the end of next March. Hythe Station is to be retained, and will become the terminus of the branch which leaves the main line at Sandling Junction. The Council have asked for an assurance that adequate bus services of the East Kent Road Car Company, with which the S.R. is associated, shall operate between Sandgate and Hythe; and Folkestone Central Stations.

The official date that the station closed was of all days April 1st 1931 after the final train leaving the station was the day before on March 31st and was driven by Mr.Sam Hall of Ashford while two guards were on the last train to say their goodbyes, they were Messrs.C.Goldsmith and H.Phillips both of Ashford.

Not long after Sandgate Station had closed, the demolition gang arrived and soon removed the buildings although left most of the track which was used as a siding from Hythe. Over the weekend of July 4th & 5th 1931, the signal box at Hythe and the No.3 cabin by the goods yard at Sandling Junction were taken out of use and from this date the line between Sandling Junction and Hythe was worked as single line.

After Mr.W.E.Harris the Hythe stationmaster retired on May 2nd 1931 the line came under the jurisdiction of Sandling Junction which led to rumours of Hythe also closing. At this time Mr. Herbert Walker, the Southern Railway General Manager said that there were no plans at present to close Hythe Station and in the following years leading up to the Second World War the short branch line received its best train services for many years. Once war broke out passenger trains to Hythe ceased and rail-mounted guns were seen on the branch with a detachment of the Royal Engineers travelling down from Kirton in Lancashire to set-up a base at Hythe. Although the short branch line did seem to manage without any great damage during the war, the parcels office at Hythe was hit by a bomb and was never repaired. In 1941 the Royal Engineers moved on to the stations at Rolvenden and Wittersham Road on the Kent & East Sussex Railway.

Although the passenger service had ceased when the war had broken out goods trains had continued and in 1942 the passenger service was briefly reinstated although on May 3rd 1943 the service was once more suspended for the rest of the war.

The Southern Railway reintroduced the passenger service to the Hythe branch on October 1st 1945 and the line continued in its own sleepy way before passing into the hands of British Railways Southern Region (BR) in 1948 after nationalisation. A deputation from Hythe met with the new owners to see if they would restore the line to its pre-war service to which BR said that it was their intention to do so although coal and carriages were a limiting factor. They were also unable to give an assurance that Hythe would remain open for goods traffic as it was now their policy to concentrate merchandise from small stations at larger railheads. A request for more main line trains to stop at Sandling Junction was turned down although BR did promise the return of a Sunday train service before the start of of the 1949 summer season. Unfortunately, despite a hot summer, the Sunday service was never restored.

In December 1949 the East Kent Road Car Co launched a new bus service between Hythe, Sandgate and Folkestone which only added to the fear of the lines future. At that time there were 33 railway season ticket holders but, by early 1950 this was down to a mere half a dozen.

After a survey was carried out by the Civil Engineering Department which stated that to keep the line open, repairs were needed at a cost of about £8,000, it was decided that the line would close on and from December 3rd 1951 with the last train running on Saturday December 1st.

On the last day a number of local people and railway enthusiasts arrived to witness the passing of this much loved line which to some locals must have seemed like losing an old friend, had it reached Folkesone Harbour as originally planned it would probably still be running. A Union Jack flag with a laurel wreath and a Hythe 'target' from one of the station lamp posts, and a notice reading 'RIP' was flown at half-mast from the parapet on the bridge at the the far end of the station towards Sandgate.

The final train arrived from Sandling Junction at 3.15 pm and was pulled by C class 0-6-0 No.31721 with a wreath made from an assortment of vegetables (ranging from carrots, sprouts, turnips, celery, hops and laurel) was added to the front of the engine on the top lamp hook. The driver was Victor Morgan, the fireman was Bob Hukins and the guard was Alex Anderson, while District Inspector Bobby Burn was also on hand to blow the final whistle to mark the last train to leave Hythe. On leaving the station the train ran over several detonators which had been placed on the track causing loud bangs and sending the train on its final journey over the short branch back to Sandling Junction.

With the remaining section of the line now closed, the dream of Sir Edward Watkin and his hope for a through route to Folkestone Harbour and the continent was well and truly over.

C class 0-6-0 No.31721 at Hythe on Saturday December 1st 1951, the last day of public service. S.C.Nash

17

Description of the Route

As we will have read in the history of the line, when the branch was first opened in 1874 all trains for Hythe and Sandgate started from Westenhanger Station on the main line towards Ashford before Sandling Junction Station was opened in 1888. From this time onwards all branch line trains started from the new junction station.

Westenhanger Station when it was the starting point for all branch trains to Sandgate (apart from any through trains of course). Once the junction station at Sandling was opened in 1888 (where the branch line actually left the main line) it soon became the lines terminus. Lens of Sutton

An early view of the station staff at Sandling Junction on the main line platform. Author's Collection

SANDLING JUNCTION STATION

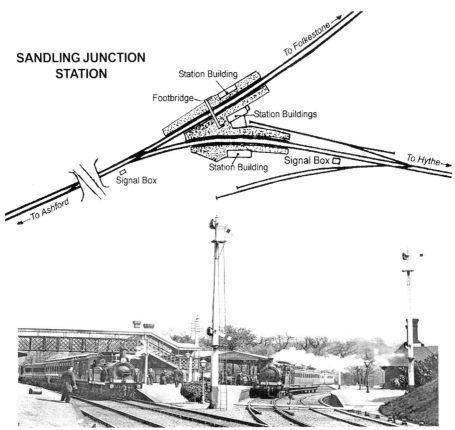

A London bound train pulled by a Q class 0-4-4T *(left)* waits at the main up platform at Sandling Junction while a rebuilt Q1 class 0-4-4T *(right)* lets off steam while waiting at the down branch platform c1907.
Author's Collection

A fast express races through the main station at Sandling Junction on August 25th 1951 while the more sedate H class 0-4-4T No.31521 waits with its train at the then single track branch line platform. R.C.Riley

The remaining branch platform at Sandling Junction looking towards the main line c1950, after the branch line had been singled in 1931. Denis Cullum

H class 0-4-4T No.31521 with branch train approaching Sandling Junction on August 25th 1951. R.C.Riley

The short Hayne Tunnel, looking south towards Hythe in 1957. R.F.Roberts

On leaving the 'down' branch platform at Sandling Junction the line dropped at 1 in 264 for a short distance before running on the level and reaching the rather impressive 94 yard Hayne Tunnel. Once out of the tunnel the line continued in a cutting while descending a 1 in 56 and passing under a three arch brick bridge which carried a bridleway from Saltwood village to a large country estate. On leaving the cutting the line passed under another three arch brick bridge which carried a footpath and soon yet another footpath was crossed but this time on the level which was protected by wicket gates. From here the line entered another cutting and passed under a brick and girder bridge which carried the road to Saltwood. At this stage the gradient dropped to a 1 in 54 and another footpath was crossed on the level while the view of the nearby Saltwood Castle must have been one of the highlights of the short journey to Hythe and Sandgate.

From here the line crossed over a farm track by another bridge and then continued into another deep cutting. The line from here ran on the level and after passing over the Blackhorse Hill Road bridge reached Hythe Station which was 1 mile 44 chains from Sandling Junction.

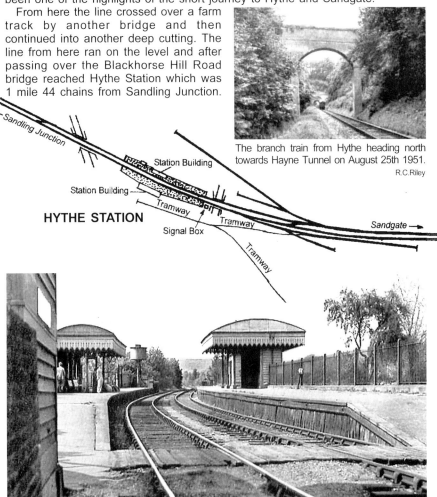

The branch train from Hythe heading north towards Hayne Tunnel on August 25th 1951.
R.C.Riley

HYTHE STATION

Hythe Station looking towards Sandling Junction in 1931.   R.F.Roberts

Looking towards Sandgate from Hythe Station in the 1920's.   Author's Collection

On leaving Hythe Station the line immediately crossed over the Station Approach Road bridge and continued on the level before dropping a gradient of 1 in 59 for about ³/₄ of a mile and passing under the Seabrook Estate bridge which carried Cliff Road. After passing the reservoir of the Sandgate Urban District Waterworks on the right side of the line, the catch points which were situated on the 'up' line for derailing any runaway rolling stock (which could have smashed into Sandgate Station) was also passed. Still continuing on the 1 in 59 drop towards Sandgate the line crossed over Horn Street on a rather grand brick bridge quickly followed by crossing over the Hospital Hill bridge and finally arriving on the level at Sandgate Station which was actually at Seabrook.

If the line had been extended to Folkestone as originally hoped, the existing station at Sandgate would have been renamed Seabrook Station and a new Sandgate Station would have been opened in a more central part of Sandgate.

The 'up' platform at Sandgate looking towards Hythe in the 1921.   John Alsop Collection

22

The station building at Sandgate soon after the train service had been withdrawn. Author's Collection

SANDGATE STATION

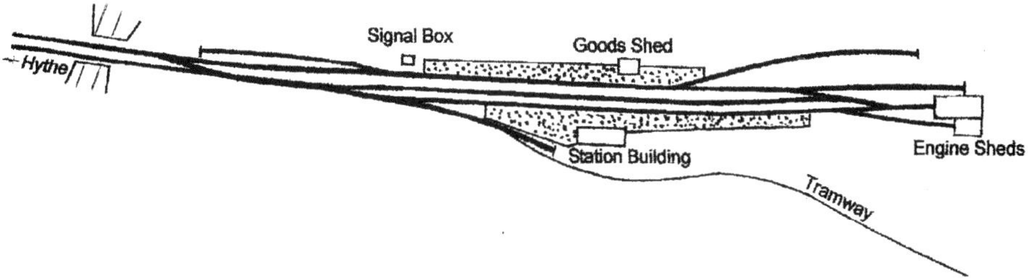
Hythe
Signal Box
Goods Shed
Station Building
Engine Sheds
Tramway

SANDGATE
PEARS
SUTTON'S SEEDS

The signal box at the end of the 'down' platform at Sandgate in the early 1900's. John Alsop Collection

Motive Power and Rolling Stock

The locomotives which were mainly used when the line first opened were Cudworth 118 class 2-4-0T and Standard Goods 0-6-0's, followed by Stirling Q and Q1 class 0-4-4T's while carriages ranged from four and six wheel non corridor stock In 1907, like many other similar branch lines in Kent it was decided to introduce Wainwright designed Steam Railcars but, as with other lines, they were not a success.

By 1916 the normal service was back in the hands of the Stirling Q and Q1's and also Stirling O and O1 class 0-6-0's, followed by the former LCDR Kirtley R and R1 class 0-4-4T's. From the 1930's, pull-and-push units were regularly in use and were worked by former London Brighton & South Coast Railway Stoudley D1 class 0-4--2T's and Billinton D3 class 0-4-4T's. The final years were in the hands of Wainwright H class 0-4-4T's. The goods traffic at this time was worked by either Stirling O1 class 0-6-0's or Wainwright C class 0-6-0's.

Cudworth 118 class 2-4-0 No.246 at Hythe after arriving from Sandgate in the 1890's. Author's Collection

Stirling O1 0-6-0 No.385 in a cutting near Saltwood north of Hythe on June 17th 1924. F.J.Agar

H class 0-4-4T No.31521 shunting in the yard at Hythe having arrived with the branch train which can be seen in the background waiting at the station platform on August 25th 1951. R.C.Riley

H class 0-4-4T No.31520 at Hythe Station in 1951, the bomb-damaged parcels office can be seen on the right of the locomotive. Author's Collection

D3 class 0-4-4T No.2365 also at Hythe in July 1938. R.F.Roberts

Timetables, Tickets and Gradient Profile

1924

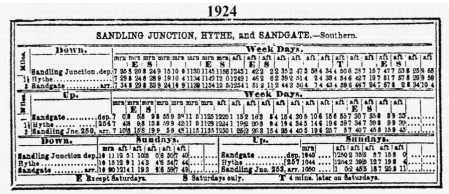

After the branch was briefly reinstated in 1942

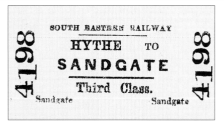

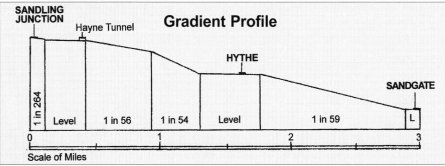

The Hythe & Sandgate Tramway

As both Hythe and Sandgate stations were inconveniently situated, a horse drawn bus service was soon introduced between Hythe, Sandgate and Folkestone although local people were not too happy about this and felt they needed something better. In 1879 a tramway between Hythe and Folkestone was proposed but was not well received by local tradesmen who were worried that they might lose business and local residents who thought that it might affect the value of their property. With this in mind, a shorter route was proposed in 1880 from the bottom of Sandgate Hill along the seafront to Hythe using horse traction.

In actual fact, a separate tramway already existed which had been built to carry materials along the new sea wall at Marine Parade (later renamed Princes Parade) designed by Sir John Coode* for the Seabrook Estate Company and was left *in situ* after the work was completed by the contractor Mr.H.B.James C.E. This existing contractors tramway gave Sir Edward Watkin the idea to purchase it and extend it with a passenger service. The idea was mentioned at a SER board meeting in April 1881 as a possible line to be built between Hythe Station and the Seabrook Hotel (opened on July 21st 1880 and owned by the SER) but because the steep gradient between the station and the town was too much for horse traction the idea was dismissed.

While designing the Marine Parade, * Sir John Coode (who was one of the most well known harbour and sea wall designers of the time) is sometimes referred to for this project as Sir John Goode which could have been confused with Mr.H.D.Good who was the Resident Engineer.

In the autumn of 1883 a nominally independent tramway company was formed and promoted by local influential businessmen Benjamin Horton, John Vallier Bean, George Cobay and Henry Mackeson and they gave the new company the full title of the Folkestone, Sandgate & Hythe Tramway Co Ltd. (FS&HT), The SER were obversely wanting to be involved and arranged for their chief engineer Francis Brady to present the FS&HT with an estimate for building the tramway. An Act was passed on July 28th 1884 which authorised the SER to work, use, manage and maintain the tramway using horse drawn traction on standard gauge track.

The tramway was in fact to be built as four sections which would all join up on completion. The first section (Tramway 1) was to run from the south side of Hythe Station where there would be a physical connection to the SER and then cross the Hythe to Sandgate Road and the Royal Military Canal finishing at the Princes Parade. The second section (Tramway 2) would run from the Seabrook Hotel along the parade as far as the Hythe to Sandgate Road junction towards Sandgate. From here the third section (surprisingly known as Tramway 4) took the line along the seafront to Seabrook on the west side of Sandgate with a spur to Sandgate Station (Tramway 4A) where like at Hythe Station it would have a physical connection. The final section (Tramway 3) would take the line to a terminus at the bottom of Sandgate Hill.

Tramway 4 had been authorised by the 1884 Act while Tramway's 1, 2 and 3 were authorised by an Act in 1886. Work on Tramway 1 and 2 got underway in 1886 under the supervision of the SER chief engineer Francis Brady who was also engineer on the construction of the Elham Valley Railway at the same time. Once these two sections of the tramway had been completed, contruction on sections 3 and 4 got under way in 1888. With Francis Brady fully involved with the Elham Valley line which was reaching its completion, he was unable to continue with the tramway so, local contractor Mr.John James Jeal who had previously undertaken building work for the SER on the Hythe & Sandgate Railway took over the supervision of the construction work.

At this stage the SER made use of some plant they had aimed to use on what would have been their Hythe & New Romney Railway and had been used on the Sudanese Railway and kept in storage at Lydd Army Camp, which also included a locomotive that had been built for the Suakim-Berber Railway which would help in laying the tramway.

With Tramway 1 and 2 completed it was time for Major General C.S.Hutchinson (formerly Colonel and incidently born at Hythe) to carry out an inspection for the Board of Trade. Major Hutchinson refused to pass the opening because of several reasons but the main one was that the first section and some of the second section were laid with rails like a conventional railway rather than rails level with the road as required in the 1870 General Tramways Act. With work on the Elham Valley now finished, Francis Brady returned to put things right but, as some requirements were on the very steep part of the line from Hythe Station to the lower town and as it was to be a horse drawn tramway, there would never be any passengers carried between the station and the town so therefore this short stretch was exempt from the Act.. Although Brady had returned he was still very much at the SER's beck and call for other projects so, Mr. Jeal remained as the contractor.

With the first two sections ready to open, work on the other two sections came to a grinding halt at Sandgate when Lord Radnor exercised a power of veto that had been included in the 1886 Act. Lord Radnor wanted to have a gauge of 3ft 6in as he felt that the streets in Sandgate were too narrow for standard gauge rails plus he also thought that the FS&HT were planning to use steam traction. The *Folkestone Express, Sandgate, Shorncliffe & Hythe Advertiser* on Saturday October 27th 1888 reported the following:-

THE HYTHE AND SANDGATE TRAMWAY

Rapid progress has been made by Mr.Jeal, the contractor, with the tramway, a large number of hands being employed on the same. Many of the public have some confused notions as to the direction which the tram will take. The line will be laid from the Hythe Railway Station on to the Seabrook Hotel, along the sea front, and will finish up at present at the Sandgate Coast Guard Station. Public opiniom in Hythe would undoubtedly like to see its convenience consulted by the tram coming from the Seabrook Hotel down into Stade Street and terminating at the Bank. As far as Sandgate is concerned, the original intension was to go on as far as the National Schools, but Lord Radnor has exercised his veto over this plan, which he is empowered to do by virtue of an arrangement arrived at between his Lordship and the Company, as explained at the Sandgate Local Board meeting on Wednesday. His Lordship objects to the width of the gauge laid down, and advises, through his agent, a three feet six inch gauge. To this, the reply is, "*that with every desire to comply with his lordship request, the company believe that a less gauge would be attended with an element of unsafety, as in the case of a gale, the car, if a larger number was sitting on one side than on the other, might possibly turn over*". At present, therefore, the tram will only be constructed as far as the Coast Guard Station, but it is hoped that in view of the representations that will be made to Lord Radnor's agent, and the probable opinion of the Board of Trade on the subject, his Lordship will withdraw his veto, and allow the work to be completed, as far as is at present designed. Some cars, on the most approved principle, are in due course being built, and as soon as ready will be tried.

By September 1889 many local people were now beginning to get impatient for the tramway to be opened, the debate between Lord Radnor and the FS&HT lingered on with letters from solicitors on both sides going backwards and forwards over the next two years. On their part the tramway company upset Lord Radnor even more when they announced that they aimed to complete the already agreed extension to the foot of Sandgate Hill and also extend west to Pennypot and then mentioned the hot potato of extending through to Folkestone via Sandgate Hill.

By this time Lord Radnor was William Pleydell-Bouverie, 5th Earl of Radnor who had inherited the title after his father Jacob Pleydell-Bouverie the 4th Earl had died on March 11th 1889.

In February 1890 it was reported that Folkestone Town Council had approved the extension into the centre of the town although the tramway company were concerned about the steep climb up Sandgate Hill plus the opposition from the influential Lord Radnor.

To avoid the situation any further, the FS&HT decided to postpone any future parliamentary Bills and continue with completing section 3 to the already authorised bottom of Sandgate Hill. At this time Lord Radnor was still insisting that the gauge was to be 3ft 6ins through Sandgate and the SER were reluctantly agreeing to build the rest of the whole line as a mixed gauge. The disagreement between the SER and Lord Radnor still continued until the quick tempered Sir Edward Watkin became so annoyed that at one stage he threatened to disband the whole tramway, as it was he ordered Mr.Jeal to begin lifting the rails in section 3.

With two new tramcars arriving (No's 1 and 2 which were ordered from G.F.Milnes & Co of Birkenhead) there seemed no point in waiting until the whole route was fully completed so, the tramway opened between the Seabrook Hotel and the east side of Sandgate on May 18th 1891. Three other tramcars (No's 3, 4 & 5) were later built and supplied from Ashford Works. Tramcar No.5 was open top and became known as the "toast rack".

At the western end of the tramway the extension to Pennypot was deferred although a new terminus was approved at Red Lion Square which was inspected by Major General C.S.Huthinson and was opened on June 1st 1892. A building close by was purchased and adapted as a tram shed while the stables and offices were located behind the shed.

After the tramway had open as far as the east side of Sandgate, Lord Radnor surprised everyone when he changed his mind and allowed standard gauge tracks through Sandgate to the bottom of Sandgate Hill. No reason was given although it does seem a coincidence that the Sandgate Hill Lift (a steep grade railway of just over 223 yards long, see photographs on page 32) was under construction at this time and its lower station would be only a short walk from the Sandgate tram terminus. Lord Radnor owned the land which the lift would run over and would receive $2^1/2\%$ of the gross takings over £1,000 per annum. For their part after Lord Radnor's late change of mind was for the SER to sign a binding agreement with him on July 14th 1892 whereby the SER agreed not to electrify the tramway at a future date.

The standard gauge tramway was soon completed to the bottom of Sandgate Hill and the first tram to run over the whole route was on July 30th 1892 followed by the full public opening on Sunday August 1st., with a half-hourly service and a tuppenny fare each way. Despite the FS&HT's title, the line quickly became know as the **Hythe & Sandgate Tramway** which meant the names Sandgate and Hythe were reversed from the original title.

A tram bound for Hythe having just left the terminus at Sandgate.   John Alsop Collection

29

On June 29th 1893 the SER obtained an Act whereby they would officially take over the whole operation and maintenance of the tramway for a sum of £29,755.

Although the SER had signed a binding agreement with Lord Raynor on July 14th 1892 it still did not stop other concerns over the next few years from attempting to do what the FS&HT had always wanted to do. One proposal which would have really helped with the linking of New Romney, Hythe and Folkestone was the Cinque Ports Light Railway in 1899 which proposed an electric light railway/tramway to run from Ramsgate in Kent, to Hastings in Sussex via Sandwich, Deal, Dover, Folkestone, Hythe, New Romney, Lydd, Rye, Winchelsea, and Pett Level. The engineers were listed as David Cook, James T. Rossiter and Mark Parker. Unfortunately, with Dover unwilling to get involved as they already had their own tramway system, this was just one reason of many that this rather adventurous scheme failed to materialise.

A report in *The Times* newspaper of May 24th 1900 mentions that at a sitting of the House of Lords committee, the Sandgate and Hythe Electric Company requested to build a tramroad from New Romney to Folkesone via Hythe and Sandgate to be worked by electricity on the overhead trolley system to prevent the long detour of 30 miles by railway from New Romney to Folkestone via Ashford at present necessary in travelling between those places. Opinion in Folkestone was favourable but opposition came from Mr. Carpenter the Mayor of Folkestone and Lord Radnor who was allowed by the committee to give his evidence:-

He said that he and his predecessors in title had taken great interest in and spent large sums in development of Folkestone as a high class residential town. If the proposed tramway entered the town it would be seriously detrimental. The cheap tripper, whom they did not want, would be brought in, and it would be impossible to maintain the high class residential character of the place.

Like so many schemes at about this time, nothing happened and these words from Lord Radnor were to be some of his last statements as he unexpectedly died on June 3rd 1900 aged 59 and was succeeded in the earldom by his eldest son Jacob Pleydell-Bouverie who became the 6th Earl and like his father, his attitude towards the tramway carried on in a similar way and even a scheme for motor trams failed to get any support.

With all the suggestions for extending in different ways and forms coming to nothing the tramway just continued in its own leisurely way under the newly formed SE&CR.

In 1914 just after the First World War broke out the tramway was suspended and its horses were requisitioned by the military authorities and the depot at Red Lion Square was believed to have been taken over by the Canadian Military Police.

Open top "toast rack" tram No.5 about to leave the Hythe terminus at Red Lion Square. John Alsop Collection

On the return to peacetime it was suggested that the tramway should be restarted, but, unfortunately the original tramway horses who were requistioned by the miitary authorities were all killed in action while abroad and no replacements were found. There was some suggestion to use motorised locomotives but this idea was quickly dismissed. To at least get the tramway moving again it was decided to use some ex Army mules who true to their name could be very stubborn but, eventually horses were obtained to replace the mules.

Once the tramway returned to normality it began to feel the competition of motorised buses and seems to have become a form of transport from a different age while running in the summer months only and mainly attracting holidaymakers more than locals.

At the end of the 1921 summer, three years after the restart, the track was in such a poor condition that during the following winter neither the SE&CR or the Sandgate UDC were interested in upgrading, so it was decided to close the line completely without any fuss.

 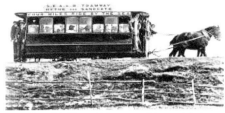

(*Left*) No 5 the "toast rack" tram and (*right*) No 3 the tram with solid sides which was mainly used during winter, both seen on the Princes Parade.   John Scott-Morgan Collection

(*Left*) The wrecked tram tracks on Sandgate Espanade after a bad storm in February 1899. Author's Collection
(*Right*) One of the open sided trams waiting at the passing loop along Princes Parade.   H.C.Casserley

No.5 at the Hythe terminus where the tram shed, stables and offices can be seen behind the tram.
Author's Collection

Sandgate Hill Lift

(*Left*) The lower station on the Sandgate Hill Lift. (*Right*) Looking down towards the lower station. This steep grade railway company was formed in 1890 with a capital of £6,000 and was just over 223 yards long and ran on a 5ft 6ins gauge. It was opened on February 20th 1893 and suspended in July 1918 due to lack of maintenance and never reopened. Author's Collection

The Present Scene

After the branch line closed in 1951 the remaining track from Hythe to Sandling Junction was thought to have been lifted in the summer of 1954 leaving just a short section of track past the branch down platform at Sandling Junction which was used as a siding, this remaining stretch of track was later lifted in the 1990's. The nearby former goods yard is now a car park where a pedestrian walkway leading to the main line station leads along the former trackbed to part of the former branch down platform. The rest of the former platform is the start of a footpath which leads up to Hayne Tunnel which is still in good condition but is several feet deep in water. From here the footpath stops and goes up over the top while although very overgrown, the route from the tunnel to Hythe can still be traced and can be seen from various other local footpaths. Although some of the bridges on the route still exists, the sites of both Hythe and Sandgate stations have since been redeveloped for housing.

Very little remains of the tramway apart from the much altered stable and office building in Rampart Road which still bares the original tram company name facia while the Tram Shed has been demolished.

Acknowledgements

I would like to thank all the people who kindly helped by providing information and photographs for this publication, unfortunately many of the photographers have now sadly passed on but, I would still like to say a big thank you to all of the names listed under the photographs.

I would also like to thank Norman Branch for reading my text, and to James Christian of Binfield Print & Design for their help.

For anyone who wants to know more about this interesting railway and tramway I highly recommend "The Hythe & Sandgate Railway" by Brian Hart which was published by *Wild Swan* in 1987.

(*Left*) The north portal of Hayne Tunnel looking towards Hythe in May 2014. (*Right*) Looking north along Horn Street in April 2014, the former Sandgate Station was 600yards to the right. Nick Catford